Turnip the Testy Turtle

Author
Marilyn Blease

Illustrator
Emre Altindag

Turnip the Testy Turtle

The day started like any other day. The sun was shining and the temperature was just right. It was just right for everyone except Turnip. You see Turnip was a turtle with a very peculiar problem. He was born without a shell.

When it rained Turnip got wet.

When it snowed Turnip got cold.

When he walked in the tall grass his belly tickled and when he walked on the rocks his belly got scratched.

You see Turnip was a little Testy. In fact that is the very way Turnip got his nickname, Testy.

On this fine shiny day, one of Turnips buddies mentioned to him about a shop down by the old branch that he just might be interested in.
The shops name was "Big Stanking Jims Turtle Emporium. Everything for the young terrapin to the old Tortoise." Well Turnip thought that it might be worth the trip to go down to Big Jims and just have a look around so off he went.

It took Turnip a while to get to the branch across the field and down in the gulley. After looking around, Turnip came across Big Jims. He got to the door and he yelled. "Hey. Anybody there?"

Big Stanking Jims
Turtle Emporium

Well from around the back of the sign Big Jim showed up. He was an old turtle that looked like he had been around awhile. Big Jim asked. "What can I do for you there little fellow?"
Well Turnip being as testy as he was snapped back. "Can't you see why I'm here! Duh. I don't have a shell!"

"Well that you don't", Big Jim replied."Well come on in and have a look around. Now, I have a pretty good shell that was traded in this week on a newer model.
Now where did I put it."

After reaching in the very back, Big Jim came out with the biggest shell Turnip had ever seen. Turnip promptly started shaking his head. "That is way too big for me. It will never fit." Big Jim just smiled and handed it to Turnip anyway and said "Try it on, you never know until you try it on and besides that's the only one I got right now."

So Turnip just did just that. He tried on that really huge shell and just as he suspected. It was way tooooo bigggg!

Turnip crawled up inside the old shell and he was able to turn comletely around and come back out. Yep, it was definitely too big for Turnip. "Well" Big Jim stated. "You right there. That thing is a tad bit too big. Come on back same time next week and maybe I will have another one for you to try."
So Turnip trudged back to his pond to wait for next week.

Sure 'nuff. Next week same time Turnip showed up at Big Stanking Jims Turtle Emporium to try it one more time. "Hello, it's me Turnip." He squeaked out. From around the sign again just like before Big Jim appeared. "Oh it's you. I'm glad you came. I have just the right shell this time I think." And with that Big Jim disappeard back in the back just as he did before. When he returned he had a shell alright. But this one was a tiny, itty bitty shell.

Big Jim boasted. "This is it, I'm sure. It belonged to a little old turtle and its hardly been used at all!"

Well Turnip took one look at it and his head just dropped. "No, no. That just will not do. It is way to tiny Big Jim." And with that Big Jim spouted out his usual comment. "Just try it on. You might be surprised."Well Turnip did just that. He squeezed his head up into that tiny little shell and his head popped out the front and his arms and legs popped out the sides. In fact, he looked like a chihuahua in a turtle neck! "Oh no! This just won't do. It is way, way too tiny", Turnip disappointingly muttered.

After repeated tries and lots of help from Big Jim, Turnip got out of the old tiny shell and agreed to try coming back just one more time.

Same time next week, Turnip showed up at Big Jims and there it was. Big Jim already had a shell out waiting. It was beautiful. It shown in the sun just like a new jewel. Turnip couldn't help but walk right up to it and touch it. "Been waiting on you. Got this little beauty in and now I know this one will fit", Big Jim proudly declared.

That it did. Turnip tried the shell on and it fit perfectly. It fit like it was made for him and with that Turnip thanked Big Jim and off he went.

He crossed over weeds that no longer tickled his belly. He walked over sticks that no longer scratched his belly. When it rained, he didn't get wet and when it snowed he didn't get cold. In fact, all of the others stopped calling him Testy. It no longer fit...

Turnip the Testy Turtle

You know, we are just like Turnip and the shell is just like a Church. We try different ones on to see if they fit and some don't. Some are too big and some are too little. You just keep trying and when you find the one that is just right for you, you will know it. It will fit perfectly!

Marilyn Blease

Made in the USA
Columbia, SC
29 October 2024

45186373R00020